This book is dedicated to Moonshine.
One of the best friends I ever had and who
taught me so much about love and forgiveness.

Illustrated by Saima Riaz

MOONSHINE SPEAKS

There is a realm of existence where all the saints, masters and angels live. It is where your soul comes from. Your soul is the part of you that makes you 'YOU'. This place is called Home. There was a wonderful, loving, powerful spiritual being living there named Kalindi. She looked down at the Earth and saw that the people could use her help to find more love and truth, so she came to Earth to help the people living here.

For a period of my life I was an assistant for Kalindi. One day she said she wanted a dog and that she wanted me to take care of it for her. The next day she came home with a cute little white American Eskimo dog and because he was white she named him 'Moonshine'.

EVERYBODY LIKED MOONSHINE !!!

Moonshine had something special. Whenever I took him somewhere he would always attract a lot of attention. People would come over and pet him. They would ask to have their pictures taken with him. Some even begged me if they could take him home and have him as their pet.

One thing about American Eskimo dogs is they are watch dogs and they are very protective of the people that care for them. Whenever anyone would come to the house Moonshine would bark to let us know that someone was there. Moonshine did not just bark. He barked and barked and barked and barked. His bark was very loud and it hurt my ears.

One day I read an article in a pet magazine about animal whisperers. These are people that are able to communicate with animals. In the article there were stories of how they would talk to the animal about behaviors they had that the owners wanted changed. When the animals understood that the owners wished for a different behavior then they would be happy to change. I prayed that someday I could meet an animal whisperer and have them tell Moonshine to not bark.

One day I was at a weekend fair with a friend of mine. Just before we were to leave she came up to me and said she had just met a woman that could talk to her cat. I asked her where this woman was and went over to meet her immediately. This woman's name is Chris. I asked Chris if she could talk to my dog and ask him not to bark so much. She closed her eyes and after a few minutes she opened them and started to talk with me.

The first thing the Chris told me Moonshine said was, *"I was with Angel in the beginning and then I was not with him for a long time. Now I am back with him and I do not want to lose him."* I was with Moonshine for the first three years of his life. After that time he went to live with a friend that was sick and needed a companion. After 5 years he came back to live with me. I had not told her anything about Moonshine but his name, where he was and what he looked like, I knew Chris was a genuine animal communicator when she told me what Moonshine said about not being with me.

It's my job!

Naturally, one of the first things I asked Moonshine about was his barking. I asked him why he barked so much and he said, "It's my job. I'm supposed to bark." I told him that his barking hurt people's ears and they got mad at me, so would he please quit barking after they come in the house? I explained to him that it was fine to let me know people were coming, but not alright to keep barking and barking and barking. He said, "Oh, that will be hard, but I will try. It may take some time though." He got much better, but then I had to go away for a month. When I came back he started his excessive barking again. When we asked him about it he said, "Well, I did what he wanted me to and then he left."

When he barked and I asked him to stop he would come over and get some rubs for doing his job well. I asked him why he did not stop when other people rubbed him. Moonshine said, "Oh, man, I will work on it, but when I bark they rub me and I like to get rubs from people."

When I first talked with the communicator Moonshine had a lot of different pains in his body. Whenever I tried to pick him up he would make a yelp. When I asked him about it he said, "I get headaches a lot. When I walk a lot my shoulders get tight and then my head hurts." We cut back on his walks and massaged his shoulders. Later when I asked him about his body he said the pain was all gone."

I asked him what he thought about Kalindi and he said, "Oh, man." She has really, really big energy. She has really strong spiritual energy." I had not told the communicator anything about Kalindi before I asked this question, so I know she did not make that up.

It was obvious to me how much Moonshine loved Kalindi. The last three times he saw her he would stop what he was doing, get on his belly and crawl to her, and then he would lie at her feet.

Moonshine had an interesting way to describe people. He did not know their names, but by what he said you knew who he was referring to. Another thing was since he was losing his sight he would describe them from the waist down. He also talked about how well he thought they would take care of him. One time I asked Moonshine about how he liked the people in the house I live in. He said, "I really like the young girl with the skinny legs that wears fancy shoes." Another time I asked the same question and he said, "I really like the girl with the fancy clothes. She always smiles when she sees me. I know she likes to take care of me."

When I asked him about two women that took care of him one time while I was away he said, "Oh, man. They treated me real special. They treated me like I was a king." He described them as 'the girl with the long legs' and the other was 'the girl that took lots of fast steps'.

Moonshine does not play with other dogs much. He seems to like the company of people more. When I asked him why he did not play with dogs so much he said, "I do not want them to know I am slower and stiffer than I used to be." I guess even dogs have some vanity.

We live across the street from a nice park in Amsterdam. One time I started the conversation by asking the communicator if there was anything Moonshine wanted to tell me. He said, "Tell him I like the park. Be sure he knows I like the park. Let him know I really like going to the park."

Moonshine used to stand on my lap and put his paws on my shoulders and lick my chin. I asked him why he liked to lick people and he said, "Well, you can hear people, you can see people, you can smell people and you can also taste people. Sometimes I like to taste people, so I lick them."

When Moonshine goes to places that have grass he likes to smell all around in the grass. Sometimes he finds something in the grass and he digs at it a bit with his paws. After he digs at it he rolls over on his back and wiggles all over the spot. I have always wondered what he was doing as I have never seen anything on these spots he rolls in. He said, "I like the smell and I want it all over my body."

One day we went on a tram ride and went walking in a large park. Later that day I talked with Chris. When I asked her to tell me what Moonshine thought about the park he said, "Today was really special. I really like this park. It is a good park with lots of new smells. I even got to ride on the tram."

I had a girlfriend in Amsterdam. When we asked Moonshine about how he felt about my girlfriend, he said, "Oh, I really like to be with her. When I am with her it feels like she is singing and even when she is not singing, it still feels like she is singing."

Moonshine really, really loved to ride in cars. He would always get real happy and pull on the leash to get to the car when he knew we were going in the car somewhere. When I asked him why he liked car rides so much he said, "When you go in a car it is like an adventure and I like adventures." Another thing was when he rode in a car he would sit up and put his ear against the seat. When I asked him why he rode in a car like that he said, "I feel a hum in the car and it goes all the way through my body. I like that."

The type of dog Moonshine is comes from cold climates, so he has really long hair. Sometimes he used to take naps in the snow when it was below 0 degrees. He gets very hot when the weather is warm. I asked him if cutting his hair helps. He said, "Yes and I really like it short on my belly. Be sure to cut the hair on my belly"

I said before that Moonshine had been worried that he might have to live with someone else again. After one haircut all his hair was growing except the hair on his back. I took him to the vet to have his health checked. We did tests and the vet said Moonshine is a healthy dog. He was always concerned he might not get to live with me. When I asked Moonshine about it he said, *"I am not growing my hair there because if Angel tried to give me away then nobody would want an old dog whose hair did not grow."* I asked him how he could stop his hair from growing. He said, *"That is my secret."* I told him I would really like it if he grew his hair back because he is such a good looking dog. He said, *"Maybe I will let it grow in a month or two."* In a month or two his hair had grown back.

I was going to be away for awhile and wanted to let Moonshine know in advance. I had arranged for him to spend some time with a friend. I explained to him that he would be spending some time with the woman that wore the white dress when we went to the beach. He said, "Oh good. I like her. She is really lively. She moves around a lot" Since he met her when we went to the beach he asked, "If I spend time with her does that mean I get to go to the beach every day? I really like the beach."

We lived in a house in Amsterdam. The Dutch houses here have very steep stairs. Whenever people from other countries come here they always ask, "Why are the stairs so steep?" One time Moonshine lost his footing and tumbled down the stairs. I was worried he may have been hurt. I called Chris to ask him if he was hurt. He said to her, "My paws hurt a bit, but I am not injured. Then he wanted to know, "Why do people build stairs like that?" I guess even dogs wonder about that too.

Moonshine was not shy about expressing his opinion. One time I asked Chris to ask Moonshine to please not bark at the people that live in the house, especially when they were just getting up in the middle of the night to go to the bathroom. He said, "It's my job. I am supposed to bark." I said I understood he was protecting me, but he did not need to tell me about people living in the house because I trusted them. Then he said, "You can't trust someone just because they live with you. I once lived with a lady that wore colorful clothes and she got in an argument with someone that she lived with and then the person moved away, so see, you can't trust someone just because they live with you. Besides if something happens then you would say why didn't Moonshine bark to tell me about this." I told him I would take that risk. He said, "Okay, I will do it, but I think you have gone mad. I think you are completely mad!!!!"

I got him a new brand of food. I wanted to know how he liked it. He said, "I like the taste and it feels better in my tummy. I can poop a lot easier too."

Sometimes we would come home and find trash all over the floor. When we asked Moonshine why he did that he said, "Sometimes I smell things that are good to eat in the trash can."

I gave Moonshine a bone right before I told him I would be leaving for a week. He said. That is Okay. I will behave. I like the people in the house. When you come back bring me a present of another bone.

Quite often after it rained Moonshine would chew on the grass. I asked him why and he said, "Because it feels good on my teeth and it feels good in my tummy". It is not because he likes the taste.

Moonshine could see angels. One time I was communicating with Moonshine through Chris and all of a sudden he said, "*There are a lot of good people that come here.*" He called them 'the shiny people you can see through'. He went on to say that when we would gather for meetings and meditations then the 'shiny people you can see through' would come and the Light around us would get bigger. Chris said he thought this was the funniest thing he had ever seen.

Moonshine started losing his eyesight when he was about 10 years old. I was able to ask him about what his vision was like. He said things in front of him were fuzzy, but he could see to the side very well. I asked him if we could find an operation that would help his eyes would he want to do it. We explained to him that he would have to wear one of those plastic cones on his head for two months and that it might be painful. He said, "I would like to see better and have more light in his eyes. I am willing to try the operation as long as it would not be a problem for Angel".

In Amsterdam everyone rides a bike. I got a bike with a basket in the front so I could take Moonshine on bike rides. At first he did not like it, but then he got used to it. He said, "I like to sit up so people will think I can see."

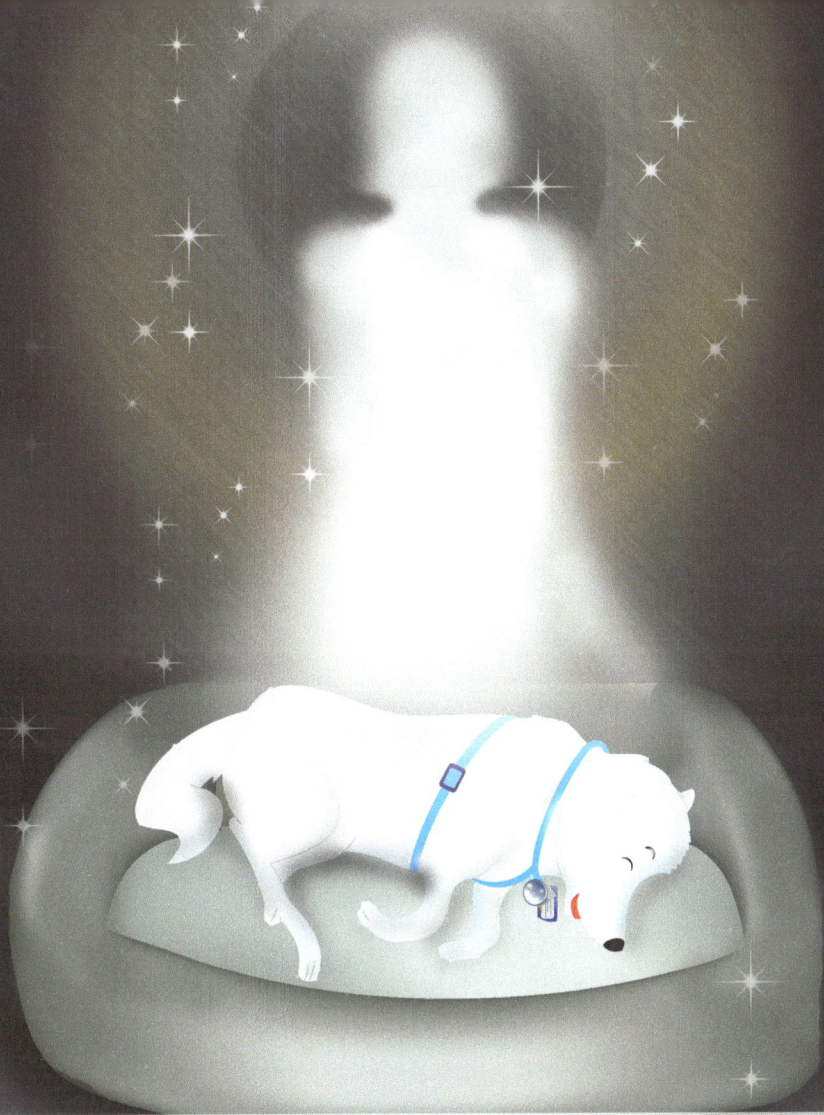

By 2011 Moonshine had gone completely blind and was almost all the way deaf. There was a change in my life and I was moving back to the USA. Moonshine could function well in our apartment, but he had great difficulty when we took him to new places. He would get very confused and unhappy since he kept bumping into things. I knew I would not be able to take him with me as I would be moving around often. I asked him if he would like anyone else to take care of him and he said he did not. I began to make plans to have him put to sleep when I left. I checked in with him regularly to see how he was doing. He said Kalindi had come to visit him when he slept and she would be waiting for him when he was put to sleep.

Even though he was almost completely deaf there was one thing he always heard and that was he always heard when someone opened the refrigerator. It did not matter if he was asleep in another room. As soon as you opened the refrigerator door you would soon hear his paws on the hard wood floors as he came out to inspect his bowl in case anyone had put some food in it.

Even though Moonshine was blind, he was not sad at all. In fact, he had a very positive attitude about everything. One time he had some trouble breathing and when I called Chris to check in with him and I asked how he was doing. He said what he always said, "I am so happy. I love my life and today was a great day!" I was very impressed that a blind and deaf dog could be so positive.

I asked him once if he had anything left he wanted to do.
Moonshine said he would like to fly. Chris explained to him that
dogs did not fly and he would have to come back to this world as
a bird if he wanted to fly. He said he did not want to fly that
much, but from then on I used to carry him under my arm and
we called that the Flying Dog position.

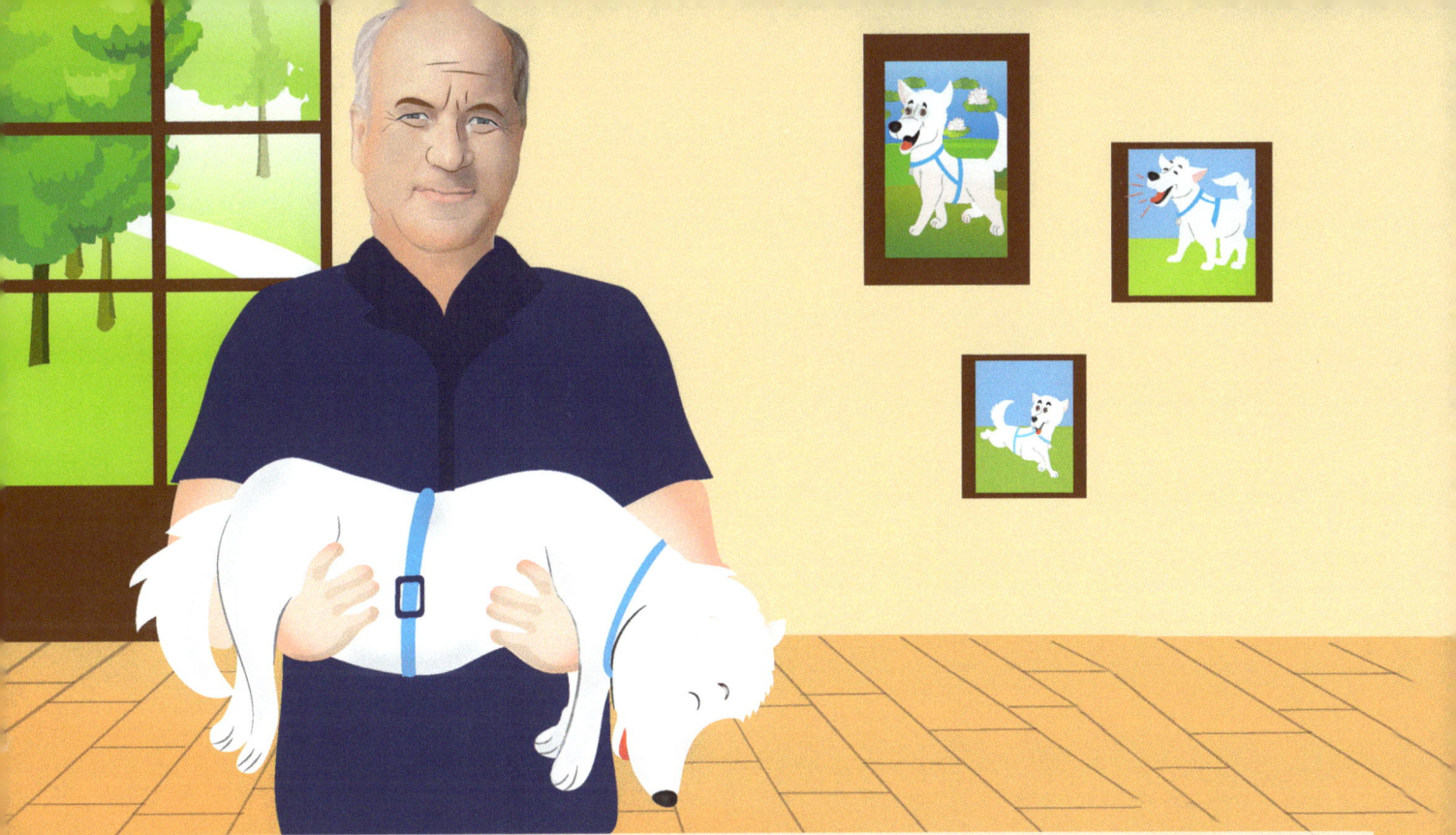

The day to put Moonshine to sleep was approaching. A couple of weeks before this was to happen I called Chris so I could talk with Moonshine. I asked him how he felt about his going to sleep permanently and he had a very interesting reply. He said, "I am ready. I could go tomorrow. I came here and I did everything that I wanted to do. I enjoyed every minute of it. I have no regrets or wishes for things to be different. I really enjoyed everything." The night before he was to be put to sleep we talked with Moonshine to ask him what he wanted. He said he did not want anything special. He wanted it to be like any other day. I did ask him if he wanted to go on one last bike ride and he said that would be very nice to do. Finally the day was here. We waited for the doctor to come to our house. I took him outside and the doctor gave him the shots to put him to sleep. I was very sad, but when I picked up his body there was no sense of anything alive in it. He was gone. Somehow the empty body made me realize in another way that Moonshine was not just a body, but the spirit inside the body.

We waited a few hours and then we called Chris to check in with Moonshine and see how he was doing after his body was put to sleep. He said Kalindi was there waiting for him and was letting him adjust to his new surroundings. I asked him if he was a dog where he now was and he said he was not. What he said is, "I am very big. I know I can shrink and fit into anything, but I still can't believe I fit into the body of that little dog."

I asked him how it was in the new place. He said, "It is nice here. There is nothing but love and peace. There is no pain and suffering, but I miss having a physical body. With a physical body you can sense beauty. I loved to feel the wind in my face, the taste of food, the smell of grass and flowers and especially the touch of people rubbing me. I cannot feel those things up here."

I asked him what it was like for him. How did he fit in with everyone else up there? He said, "*It is too hard to explain to humans what HOME is like.* I asked him what he was. There was a long silence and then he said, "*I am one of Kalindi's helpers.*" Those words rang loud and clear to me. He came here because he loved Kalindi and wanted to be near her while she was on the earth. Now after he died he continued to help her. I never asked him another question.

Moonshine Mantra

Moonshine was very positive and happy. That is one reason people liked him so much. If you would like to feel how positive and happy Moonshine was, then you can do the Moonshine Mantra. Just keep doing it until you have a smile on your face and in your heart so you can be positive and happy too !

Say it.   Sing it.   Feel it.   Think it.

Moonshine Mantra
I am really happy.
I love my life.
Today is a great day.

You can also make up your own words from your heart about how good you feel, how much you love your life and how positive today and everyday is. It is helpful ! ! !

3 months old

3 months old

Moonshine with Angel

Moonshine before a trim

Moonshine after the trim

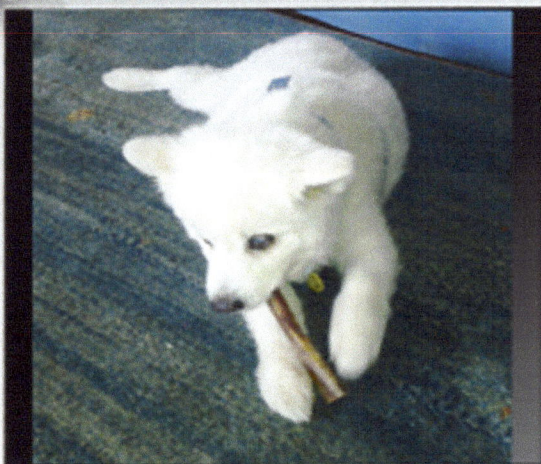

Chewing on his favorite
chew stick

At the North Sea

Moonshine and Angel on bike

Moonshine with friend

Moonshine sleeping
on couch

Moonshine up close

www.ingramcontent.com/pod-product-compliance
Lightning Source LLC
Chambersburg PA
CBHW042001100426
42813CB00019B/2951